The Madhouse System

Graham Allen

To Tim & Ruth
Best wishes
Graham

Published in 2016 by
New Binary Press
Cork city, Ireland

www.NewBinaryPress.com

ISBN 978-0-9935803-1-4

Cover by Goran Jovanovic-Boskovic

New Binary
Press

for my son, Matthew

Acknowledgements

With thanks to those editors who have published these poems in the following journals:

‘Torn’ in *Southword*
‘Drunken Song’ in *The Ogham Stone*
‘Lotus’ in *The Penny Dreadful*
‘How to improve your sleep’ in *Other Poetry*
‘The Purpose of Love Poetry in Twenty-First Century Ireland’ in *The Weary Blues*
‘Stepping Stone’ in *Gadabout*
‘Trojan Horse’ in *Burning Bush 2*
‘Divorce’ in *Stony Thursday*
‘Bright Star, Elegy for David Bowie’ in *The Bogman’s Cannon*
‘Not You’ and ‘Sydney Park, Spring 2015’ in *Poetry Ireland Review*
‘Head Down’ and ‘Parkinson’s Disease’ in *The Quarryman*

A selection of these poems was shortlisted for the 2014 ‘Fool for Poetry’ chapbook competition.

Thanks to Roy Sellars, Carrie Griffin, Jimmy Cummins and James O’Sullivan for reading versions of this book. For other gifts of reading thanks to Kevin Griffin, Anne Fitzgerald, Mary O’Connell, Liam Lenihan, Sarah Wood, David Coughlan and Rachel MagShamhráin.

Contents

The Spells

The Madhouse System

If the fool would persist in his folly he would become wise.

William Blake, *The Marriage of Heaven and Hell*

Spoiler Alert

We didn't win the day.
The heroine died.

The promising sidekick,
whose wine-dark hair

glistened attractively in the breeze,
tripped on a paving stone.

Every one that had access
to the seventeen digit

closely encrypted emergency security code
released their weapons.

The thin interstellar signal,
sent with great hope and hospitality

throughout the vastness of space,
remained unanswered.

The man with generous eyes
and a noble forehead,

reminiscent of your father's,
wept into a small bowl of cold soup.

Sydney Park, Spring 2015

We are coming to the end of winter.
Folds of steam are swagging up

from the river-hugging, splintered town.
The sun is returning.

Light is welling, spreading
itself like water fills a tank.

Along the footpath and the walled house gardens
a thousand things I have no words for

are being born.
I am no field botanist, gauging

the heliotropic scene.
I am not Adam in Paradise

confronted with the nameless beasts.
I am a survivor of the unspecified worst,

surprised by my own persistence,
shocked by contingency,

the last guy standing as the credits come down
at the end of an old disaster movie.

If not from scratch, then still, somehow,
we are going to have to start over again.

The Madhouse System

Once captured, I was in the hands of those whose interest it was to ruin me bodily and mentally.

Richard Paternoster, *The Madhouse System*

My father put me in a madhouse,
Finch's on the Kensington Road,
he said I sailed too close to the moon,
but he wanted my money.

If you could see what I have seen,
English Bastilles, madhouse dungeons,
you would think yourselves less secure
from the bloodied hands of evil men,
the proprietor doctors, the twisted priests,
the warders, half-mad dogs themselves,
all the agents of the Lunacy Laws
that mock our boasted liberties.

Poor Châteauroux threw a bone overboard
and got pinched to within half of his life.
Mr Andrews, who would stand on his tiptoes,
got a fist full of cayenne pepper to choke.
Robert Orme Smith lived thirty years sane
in Warburton's Asylum, Bethnal Green.
Lady Kirkwall was bricked up by her sons
who rioted after on her estate.

Look at that giant iron cage
that keeps a man still for twenty-four hours,
look at those men, heads strapped to their beds,
too frightened to shit or piss in relief.
Doctor Munro keeps a man down for years,
releasing him finally into God's arms,
gets paid an annuity for every one,
avoiding the pauper dead souls and true fools.

Captain Saumarez saved his brother
and we founded the Alleged Lunatic's Friends,
but our families hover above us like carrion,
and the industry thrives, and the last light fades.
In Munro's Brookhouse, Upper Clapton,
the Misses Pettingal rule the roost,
and beyond the green marsh exercise yard
stands the Dantean house of correction.

Let me describe your nation!

Husbands incarcerate their wives,
wives in turn sell off their husbands,
hired informers cash in rumour,
while brother against brother rages
through the land, where money kills nature,
all blood bonds and justice;
vigilant, mad doctors line the horizon.

The Second Law

You came late to this,
ploughed other adjacent fields,
until the time arrived.

Now there's a hole in your brain,
a question mark on your chart,
a comma that's lost its tail.

The only route out of this
is the only route out of everything.
People will speak of positive thinking,

sprouting idiot cant,
eulogising modern pharmacy,
but it is you

trapped in a car with no brakes
speeding down the motorway
towards an unknown toll bridge.

It is you
sealed inside an abandoned ossuary,
slapped flat into the face of entropy.

The wisest will ask
what's the difference?
You will have no reply,

save for the assertion that there is one.
You will know from now on
who your friends are,

as you continue, testament
to the second law
and the on-coming triumph of the real.

You are quietly being torn,
atom by atom,
stretched out on the rack

of life's own auto-immunity,
like everyone and everything else.
They will not thank you

for pointing this out,
that darkness has already won
and just needs to claim its prize,

that nothingness
need not compete
with the impotent world of things.

They will call you names,
fixing you with medical tags,
placing you on the periphery,

like a dog that will not stop barking,
or a distractible child at school,
but from now on you are a marker

of the abysmal plughole of Necessity,
the inability of chance
to act the super-hero,

or at least stop the sluice-gate
from swallowing the whole caboodle,
hungry open maw that it is,

everything slipping down,
all head first heading southwards,
slip sliding down the hole of the future,

down the twisting funnel of fate,
only you going faster than the rest,
a school kid on a diving board showing off.

Geneva

after Mary Shelley

The mountain finds its double
in the mirror of the lake.

Some birds fly south,
some birds fly north.

Rousseau lived, thought and died here.

My mother was the daughter
of my father's friend,
my future wife was my cousin.

I love my family
and read all the books that are taboo.

Electricity opens the sky,
blasts the tree to a stump
and illuminates the mountain summits.

I fly kites during storms
and consider revolution,
its degrade and its folly,
the imbalances involved in man.

Cornelius Agrippa drank
the elixir vitae and lost his reason.

Paracelsus taught
an abortion to speak Greek.

Albertus Magnus traced
the contours of the human mind
concluding it aporetic.

One day I will open the book
that no one has yet learnt to read,
the book made of the softest vellum
written before the invention of ink.

One day I will read that book,
with its promise of freedom,
equality, friendship;
one day, when I have learnt the gentle,
generous art of storytelling.

Curiosities

Here there is a madman's tongue,
a key to a wooden box full of secrets,
the toughened liver of an executed boy,
a black dog made from Arabian horse hair,

a silver hand glass without reflection,
a baby that neither wakes nor sleeps,
ceramic pill boxes full of relics,
fingernails, golden teeth, conical locks,
one ear the shape of Madagascar,
a dimpled chin with a black pearl stud.

Here there is a severed hand,
three silver rings on three straight fingers,
the glistening blue foetus of a sperm whale,
the dried scalp of an ignorant man.

Here there is a bag of cat's eyes,
a large white bowl full of frozen lizards,
and a leather book that moans and moans
about a villain who is off the hook.

Here is the world's *Wunderkammer,*
a minute lunatic archaeology.

Here is the girl with the head deformity,
six outrages terraced from her spine,
the wild mushroom flattened faces,
the orgiastic herbarium spores.

Here are the orange South Sea sponges,
the seahorse horns fashioned into frames,
one green fin as large as a table,
one Narwhal tusk as large as a door.

Here is the single bronzed and jewelled breast cup,
black square basalt from Grímsvötn lake,
the double helix egg from Baton Rouge,
the miniature phallus on a porcelain mount.

This is the stuffed pig of Geok Tepe,
who carried the word hoard over the mountains.
There is the mask of Eshu Elegbara,
hung for divination from a wooden stick.

Here is the spectre glass free for inspection,
the padded envelope with the scream inside.
Here are the lips that smack and chatter,
the body suit of skin the poet sloughed off.

Here is the sheep's skull complete with calculus,
the dragonhead mask with piano key teeth,
the unpredictable Chinese phoenix,
the bird beak tweezers, the bird beak wand.

Here is a swollen pock-marked globe
filling the windows with its own orange light,
casting long shadows across the cabinets,
the moon is landing! the moon has arrived!

Creatures

It is said that the dog men
of medieval book and lore,
who once proudly ploughed
the fields of Northern Europe,
their hands calloused
with honest, agrarian labour,
unwilling subjects of heated
scholastic dispute,
sequestered themselves away
under the hills of the evergreen West,
until they were forgotten,
wiped clean away
from all theological questions,
the great link ladder from Heaven
pulled from under their feet,
consigned to myth like the crow head,
the fish mouth and stick men
who have eyes inside their own chests.
Left alone to sing their songs,
to raise their children, and to nurse
their own fantastic stories
of beautifully formed alien
creatures with angelic faces
and genocidal minds.

Drunken Song

A large black dog in the near distance
regards you as you struggle
to stand still against this dark wall
of you do not know where or what;
people may be about to reappear,
your nose may well be a fountain,
there is something wrong with your feet,
your ankles have been stolen,
no more revelation from there.
The earth is moving very quickly now
and the moon is full of goodbyes,
quietly loosening the knots from its wrists,
leaving the oceans to their own devices.
Maybe when it's gone the poles will flip,
snap back like a heavy sprung door,
and the earth will become an ash-tray,
winter all winter, summer all summer,
the trees forgetting how they ever grew,
and you will gradually dry out
and learn to stand alone and not crumble.

Stonework

for John W. Phillips

i

Coming out of Heuston Station, Dublin,
going south, not years, five months ago,
you were still so full of words not spoken,
but something sifted you like soil in a sieve,
and all that remains is stone hard and jangling.
Put all those pebbles in a small tin box,
Sellotape down the lid and shake.
That is your gift, your palinode, your hymnal,
your less than organic contribution.

Empty, no relay, nothing can come …
a clump of unborn words in you,
a clog of black hair mass in a pipe
suspended, the house unvisited,
roof and guttering long fallen.
The rain comes and gathers and spills,
the lead slowly turns to orange,
then red, then ash black, sharp
to the touch, universal in decay.

A stone dropped into a well,
long dry of use, bone hole,
resounds and resounds and resounds,
Echo calling out his name,
side bouncing off side, and again,
until you could almost imagine
there was never any stone
in the first place, no woman in love,
in vain, not even any well itself,

just sound, nothing will come …
a name that does not give

or take, unrecorded in the minutes,
a secret, not something that could be called,
told, catalogued, ordered about,
a birthmark on the inside of the hand
no one will ever see, a comfort stone
kept in the pocket of your long coat,
something to get you through the winter.

Size of the world in the hand
of a god. More than one poem
on the subject of. Nothing can come …
smoothed by ten trillion waves,
its contours countless, its colours
unmatchable, it rests, cool,
perfectly sculptured, in the palm
of your fist, inside your great coat,
gifting you ground and centre.

Turn to symbol and murder,
or keep in the smooth round hole
of your hand, feel the energy
of millions of years of speechless motion,
thoughtless revolution, carbon life,
adaptation, always adaptation,
mineral life, every journey to England
ever made and back again.
In the last act that stone in your pocket,
keeping you alive and focused.

ii

Back to tell the tale, or lie,
communicate a pile of ashes,
where there should be sequence,
trailing your finger through those fine grains,
making enigmatic symbols
on the road down which processions came,
the horses shaking them out of her box,
unremarked numbers, hexes, signs
of a story you cannot now recall.

Quietly I have returned,
aware now of the surrounding silence,
aware now of the life of the earth,
the pace of its corruption, loneliness
of its making, and its unmaking,
the time that the fly sprints out
of its decay, the time of her mouth,
the words she will not now say,
the duration of what there is yet to know.

The time of all the rings, tree, church,
mountain, lake, the love of the moon
for the oceans, the love of the oceans
for her and him. The time of all debts,
deliveries, betrayals, unnecessary deaths.
The time of the impossible,
that which can never be born,
that which can never be said.
Aware now but not able to tell,
standing mouth agape on egg shells.

iii

You have returned with silence, bar a word
which murders and creates.
One word, with two faces, like a coin
you might flip testing Fortune.
The face they make together cannot be said,
seen, painted, kissed. You have returned
to tell him he is dead but that
already out of his unclosed eyes
spring intoxicating flowers.

You have returned to show her
the plant that unfolds in sweet leaves
out of her abdomen, elaborate
asphodel, *kat' asphodelon leimôna.*[x]
The land that was a prison, a ship,
a rotten stage, a purse with small change,
is growing a summer beard of moss,
nettles and weeds from its forgetfulness,
everywhere meadows of those sad spectres.

This is where ghosts live. We are
ghosts, *kat' asphodelon leimôna.*
The thin man shovels, but the ground
is granite. There is nowhere to bury
our dead. Nowhere to lay our heads.
Caught in the gap between life and death,
biding our time, we cannot get
under the earth or back into the stars,
marooned on a sliver of rock.

You have returned to say this thing,
to set it down in the minutes.
Suspended between these two faces,
knowing as you do their mutual
regard, unable to settle on one.
Asphodel field, nothing can come …

Speak again. Knowledge in duration.
Out from her lips which you never kissed
came strange flowers from a legendary island.

[x] kat' asphodelon leimôna (through the meadow of asphodel); 'kat' asphodelon leimôna (through the meadow of what remains unburned). See John W. P. Phillips, 'Asphodel and the Spectral Places', in *Where ghosts live*, *Derrida Today* 5.2 (2012).

Stepping Stone

Improbable stone flung into the sky,
your face lost out to a bullet-shaped hole,
without you loneliness would kill us,
wandering ghosts in the shadowless dark.

Blake raised a ladder up to your arc
fixing you like a giant kite.
Will you take us with you when you go?

I think of you as a displaced angel,
inscrutable, bewildered, prone,
inching back from the storm out of Eden,
hungry for exit music and credits.

Scientists and poets feed on your smile,
home-base for the big push up to the stars,
your violence made us seasonable,

apocalyptic coitus churning the soil.
Skimming stone illuminating the clouds,
we should have stood you for the sun,
open to every metaphor we have.

That trick you have of being double,
lying fagged out in your own new arms,
we need you to teach it to us again.

Only the True Gods Bleed

The lights are fading,
Churchill style.
The sun dips behind the western hills.

You can do nothing about this.
You are an unused sub
on the bench

as your team takes a beating.
They say use your imagination,
reality will conform,

but that is a lie. Slowly
you have realised,
there is no hope from there.

Let go of the rock
and it falls. Release
your grip, the paperwork flutters.

Stand absolutely still,
a picture of concentration,
Earth continues to flash through space.

The world lives by its own laws.
All poets are dreamers.
There will be no help from them.

Force your way up Mount Helicon,
the fact remains, that if
'all deities reside in the human breast,'

and if by the human breast
we mean the human heart,
and if the human heart is not made of stone

but made of flesh,
then that is a porous
platform for creation.

For you, who will never read
the star map of Moses Cordovero,
or hold a piece

of the broken vessels of Masada,
there will be mysteries
that remain unmastered,

questions which remain
questions, such as
where have you come from?

and, what is it you have forgotten?
and, most importantly of all,
where is it you think you are going?

The Trout of Acceptance

The quarter-life crisis sneaks up on the mid-life
and your appetites collapse like an old detonated

1960s cooling tower leaning over into the abyss
of nothing and no returns and the booze is your belly

the music all retro plastic nastiness and celebrities
celebrities because of being stupid and you find yourself

snatching for the remote and shouting out abuse
at the six o'clock news which is full of distant wars and idiots

in session and people who once hosted chat shows
with what were once opinions and weather girls with miraculous
teeth

and politely revealing summer dresses full of apologies
because the oceans are too fat and you retreat to your laptop

access to the web which is full of someone else's medicine
with advice on easy living attractiveness friendship power sex

cool labour practices how to photograph the elderly
and sixteen ways of locking up your conscience in impregnable
shackles

of improbable hysterics and fathomless faith and the typos
and misprints linguistic infelicities brutalised Americanistic
grunts

and splutters of all such gurus and honest Joes and Johannas
despite the ubiquity of spell-checks university degrees and
opportunities

we never had as children makes you shout out again at the
impassive flat screen tottering like dinner on your unsteady lap as
the edge of the world

shadows into view with the sun's decision to hide behind
the carpet and the garden shed you have once again forgotten
to maintain

and you say to yourself as you disconnect from that world of
grinning smugness that these are not your people your problems
or your answers

and that beauty still remains quivering like a beached brown trout
with little trust in the help of the tide on this particular evening

waiting to be picked apart by the sword beak of hungry seagulls
dreaming about legs and next week's sushi fish bar menu . . . .

Celtic Twilight

The stars have all gone out in your face.
The tide in your smile has waned.
All the poets have left your mind
and relocated to sunnier climes.
Your rational faculties have been paid off
and have accepted early retirement packages.
You appear to have run out of umbrellas.
Anything valuable you saved from the storm
has been transferred to an undisclosed tax haven.
Your hands are blunt hammers.
Your political agents are cold cigarette butts.
Your always unsteady sense of responsibility
has been taken over by a European department.
You have begun, that is to say, to rust.
Car alarms erupt as you walk past.
Birds skulk and then fly from your gaze.
The Fates deny all knowledge of you.
You glance at the religious and they lose faith.
You touch the athletic and they limp away.
Black dogs cross the street to avoid you.
Idealists weep at the sight of your shadow.
Children confuse you with the Bogey Man.
History has cut you from its Christmas card list.
Karma has unfriended you on Facebook.
Without exaggerating the point, you've changed.

The Enlightenment

A car alarm
accidentally triggered
in the middle of the night,
as you try to sleep.

Letter from an Irish Poetry Publisher

I have read through that volume
it took you years to write,

the one you sweated blood for,
the one that cost you your wife,

that pensionable job,
peace of mind, all confidence,

and I cannot find one line
that speaks to me of anything other

than you and your unspecifiable
disappointments. There is no music,

no lyrical voice, no signature, no tone,
in any of it; the distant hillsides,

recalcitrant children, the yappy dogs,
the constellated sprays of stars,

all the lonely women and all the lonely
men you have locked and twisted

into clinches seem false and ugly
and not worth your own

or anyone else's attention. If the book
were larger, I'd use it as a doorstop

or paperweight for my accounts.
But it is thin, blunt, tired,

and of no utility whatsoever.
We'll definitely take it!

The Nightmare

after Mary Shelley

Her hair falls over her face amending the reference,
improving the symbolism, but her eyes have gone.
Sudden nightmare, worse than what had been born
and was ever only bearable, came out of the darkness
into which he disappeared. Secrets were revealed then,
but not in the manner of truth and not so that they
could ever be understood; secrets turned to an event
she will never now assimilate. One face that stuck to her eyes
moved forwards and then closed them tight.
One face she did not know and could not place,
with something in its look like vengeance, or pity,
emotion beyond her ken, like a want she had seen in others
but never felt in herself. One face which arrived
unannounced, tearing the veil of silence and unknowing,
from that other world he had kept her from,
unholy, unspeakable, reeking of impropriety,
the midnight scalpel, the tang of blood and kisses,
all the quick, hot, feeding world of the open cadaver,
coming in through the window, still barred to her and her kin.
One face she did not know, arriving here and now, this night,
on this of all nights, witness to an unknown life
and the ending of hers. . . .

Not You

Tonight there is defeat.
The moon is absent.
Nothing fits.

Across the landing
people you will never know
are screaming at each other.

The radio news counts numbers
of unemployed,
the t.v. is full of junk.

The novel you selected
and positioned on the table
is too painful to commence.

You have not met your daughter
for six whole months.
Nobody calls.

The notebook you bought last week
is empty,
save for five aborted lines.

The internet is down,
your limbs creak,
your lips are cracked, lacking balm.

That photograph of yourself
hours before graduation
is no longer representative.

You have forgotten everything
you ever knew about the fossils
arranged on the mantelpiece.

Outside the house, beyond
the constant traffic, someone,
not you, is looking at the stars.

What Falls

The woman with no mouth
in a Bank of Ireland blouse
holds up a list
of barely readable
subsistence rates
drawn up
by a professional man
from Trinity College, Dublin.

Light from a top window
slants into the office
like sand poured from a jar,
or an old movie projector,
or rays of the sun slicing through cloud.
This is free, uncosted,
extra to economy.

But what about chance,
accident, contingency?
The stuff life throws at you?
The blows you just cannot duck?
A long, slender finger,
crimson gloss newly applied,
points to the list.
That's all factored in, she hisses.

There are no Storms in Cork

for Colm Murphy

For a whole week
the air has been wet,

sodden, like the inside
of a cloud,

or the heavy weight
of a saucepan lid.

Something needs to break,
but if not the weather

then what? our hearts?
our minds? our promises?

our willingness
to push forward?

our memory
of how all this arrived?

our faith in something
beyond the aleatory?

The rain stops,
we venture from our houses.

As I walk our future,
asleep in his buggy,

up and down Wellesley Terrace,
fiddles and drums

seeping from historical windows,
something like lightning

flashes for one time only
way off in the West.

Politician

You are a cipher, an egg-shaped zero,
less than useful, more than useless,

your mother would not credit you,
you are an expensive national joke,

a lie against every decent value.
The tears you create you do not see,

the pain you promote occurs in bodies
you will never stand beside or touch.

Nothing brings you to account.
Your tongue is a blunt stick of splinters,

your eyes are holes where moss has taken,
your brain is a bucket full of wasps,

everything you finger turns to pus,
every flash of your brain is a suicide.

Your plans are a pile of unsteady bricks,
your hopes are shit smeared across a windscreen,

your big idea is a still-born foetus
slipping out of a black refuse sack.

The promise of election drags at you
like a Hoover pulls in a spider's web,

but you have seen who is really in charge
and it's left you blind, clueless, flaccid.

Speak into the camera now with a smile
and scripted words that stick on your lips,

promote big business, taxation and war,
crude marionette with visible strings.

Say phrases like *there's no alternative*,
and *what people really need to understand*,

and, most of all, *this hurts us as well*,
then go home and do not wake your children.

Drink from that bottle behind the cabinet,
as your wife dreams of other men,

and sink into the consoling thought
that somebody has to do these things.

The Return

No other Odysseus will ever return to you.
That man and I are one, the man you see ….

The Odyssey, Book 16

Greek

Do not look for me in the mountains or the forests,
everybody will know that I have gone.

Most will not care, though some will tell stories
of golden birds, battles, staged heroic deaths.

Credit who you will, but largely stay silent,
rest upon the knowledge that this itself will pass.

Avoid excessive hope, indulgent despair,
create nothing more for them to annihilate.

You will know in your heart when you find me.

Trojan Horse

We left Fallujah in the evening,
gun fire cracking in the distance,

a ragged army of spectres,
stealing down broken streets,

dreading the idea of return.
Our memories on lock down.

The atrocities we had witnessed,
the carnage we had engineered,

left for the locals to pick through.
Our route was northwards to Mosul,

leaving the Euphrates for the Tigris,
out of the plain that had been Eden

before the fact and legacy of Cain.
Fa-lal-lujah to the tune of Leonard Cohen

as night condensed us into sound,
a battalion of hopeless fireflies,

devoid of gifts, stories or insight,
thwarted Magi relinquishing the quest.

I thought of meeting my boy again,
how his mother might resent the years,

home now a hollow sounding word,
after the limbs, the car bombs, the rockets,

charred bodies, the agony of fire on skin,
the endless nights of vigilance and fear,

and I knew I would have to wander the earth,
find a more meaningful quest,

before I could breathe clean air again,
or bear the look in his bright blue eyes.

Black Home

These are the words we can think of to utter.
This is the time we are living in now.

An Arctic wind blows down the Roman Road,
segues through the pawn shops and enters your heart.

No one bothers about the fattened ghosts.
Decrepit crones inch forward in their buggies.

Hoodies dart in and out of the dark.
The stench of disappointment rises from the gutter.

That man is a racist and a public servant.
That policewoman is bullied by her boss.

Celebrity culture is raging, sovereign,
everyone transfixed by a shabby detail.

The imagination is that ability of yours
to conjure up at any moment the worst.

A jet plane crashes into an office block.
Guards with heavy weapons break into the house.

Lightning eradicates the future.
Drones seek out your sister and your son.

Somewhere in the foothills of Afghanistan,
two hundred years after sallies with the Brits.,

unregistered, unnoticed, as you leaf
through jazzled t-shirts hung up in a stall,

your only son takes a bullet in the helmet,
imagining your thin fingers as he drowns.

Nobody

You cannot speak for me and mine,
you were not there, you have no clue.

When we hid in the darkness,
the open eye of fire upon us,

was it you whose itch unleashed
a volley into Roberts's head and chest?

Was it you who stayed McCready's arm,
ready to launch a rescue flare?

Was it you who found the unbolted door
into the factory maze and silence?

And is it you who day-dreams carnage
in imagined streets, where you were never posted?

Is it you who hears the voices of the dead
as cooked pork wafts down unwashed corridors?

Is it you who waits, scrubbed clean, every day
for visitors who will never arrive?

And is it you with your easy outrage,
your eloquent camaraderie,

who lives with a brutal one-eyed creature,
hopeless of sleep or a proper name?

Hades

I returned a blind man,
my hair white and knotted,

signs of death around my eyes.
Every vision I had seen,

every spectre I had conversed with,
mythical women, once heroic men,

oceans of the defeated,
hissing from centuries of dying,

all the philosophy I had received,
left me on my return to the sun.

Flashes of children tied to corpses,
women with wombs egg-shelled empty,

desperate men gnawing on skulls,
detonated inside my mind.

I cannot tell you how it goes there,
though I have spoken with the dead.

I cannot tell you if pain is suffered
in that place that is still burning.

I cannot pronounce on love or knowledge,
though I have walked the underworld,

wandered along its riverbanks,
smelt the scent of its loveliest flowers,

studied its half-lights and its colours.
I cannot tell you what happiness

and what misery wait for you there,
how loss of the sun is born by men,

if poets there write elegies
apostrophising the absent moon,

whether people sing of the old lands,
in melodies composed on earth,

flooding the afterlife with nostalgia,
an impenetrable fog of hopeless desire.

Nothing from there is ever recovered,
save the lingering idea of return.

Divorce

She is sending you out into the night
like a dog that has lost its reason,

a ghost unable to rattle the windows
or raise a shout from the moon-struck wolves.

Somewhere at the back of the garden
everything you ever owned is burning.

Somewhere in a trail of grey dust
lie all the stories you thought you had secured.

This is the holocaust of your existence,
a ripped out page in an unread novel,

deleted snaps of a birthday party
you were never invited to,

an indecipherable scribbled note
inside the red recycling bin.

The son who mourned when you shipped out
has almost forgotten your face.

History Class

His father is still returning
from the invasion of Eden,

his teacher lyrically declaims
on manifest destiny.

The words he writes in his copybook
are in such tiny letters

that no one, not even he himself,
will ever be able to decipher them.

After school he wanders the streets
imagining reunions. Grandparents

talk about the Blitz as if the bombs
had never stopped falling.

They wear thick spectacles
through which to see their younger selves.

Rocky the dog is old and sick
and waits all day at the bay window.

He wants to be the first to spot
his owner's re-entrance into the world.

The son takes a tennis ball into the street
and throws it for an hour against a wall.

When his arm grows tired he slopes home,
the pull of homework dragging at his feet.

Lotus

As soon as we arrived I knew that everything was broken.
There was no need for catalogues, no lyrical anaphora

of that and this and over there. The core of the place
had been gutted. You could see it in every face,

every pair of listless eyes that met us on the beach,
every hiss and giggle from the hoopla girls,

the way some had been slapped short by time.
We dragged the boat onto the coarse sands

and started to make enquiries. What happened here?
How many are already dead? Is anyone in charge?

But all that returned were grins and muffled curses,
languid stares, a sullen refusal to communicate.

An elderly woman wept into our questions.
Penned in by zombies and idiot children,

our ghoulish, lumbering, welcome party,
we pushed up to the nearby fields beyond

an innocent wall of dunes. It was then I smelt it,
the dense, complex, resinous stench of freedom.

State

Something was broken from the beginning,
something that led to this chaos in the sun.

They thought they were eliminating danger
by levelling houses and mosques with shells.

They turned towns into rubbish heaps
where old women cut their feet hunting for water.

Now people pick for food amongst ruins
and fascist opportunists beat our children to death.

Many, half crazed, turn to talk of 'the infidels',
I say talk is cheap, human life cheaper.

I say this country can never be America
and is now strip-mined of all its worth.

The liberation tanks have long been airlifted,
leaving us, food for the ravenous hawks.

If my sons returned now, pining for their nation,
they would scoop up ashes from the levelling sands.

Lost

She only knows that his body came home
but that his mind did not. The core

of him tossed out of some truck,
baked to a stone in the desert sun.

They come to lift him into the bath
twice a week, heavier each shift,

a big, bruiser, ex-paratrooper,
all muscle and fat, but no light.

She feeds him by way of conversation
and watches him stare down the day,

motionless, in his favourite chair,
seeing beyond her delicate nets,

beyond the street that welcomed him home,
beyond the games of neighbouring kids,

to a slumped decapitation, heavy with child,
some squaddies kicking her football head.

Head Down

They turned you into a photograph,
an image of damage,

and everyone who had ever had a child,
or ever been a child, mourned.

People spoke of outrage, betrayal,
charity and war.

The internet buzzed,
and pulsed, and crackled.

Prayers were raised,
analyses delivered.

Everyone opened their eyes,
extended their vision,

considering the homeless,
the exiled, the dispossessed.

But nothing changed,
and nothing ever will.

The Spells

.... to hope till Hope creates
From its own wreck the thing it contemplates....

P. B. Shelley, *Prometheus Unbound*

Branches

for Dad

These hills were new when you were young,
bright white pyramids circling Whitemoor,

now your three sons accompany you home
they are naturalised with grass and gorse.

No one need know they were dug from the earth,
Cornishmen being natural diggers,

the original miners with their own diaspora,
scattered to the black mining holes of the globe.

Because I am your son I have kept this place inside me,
like a face I never knew how to put on,

like a home I have never been able to live in,
a disused tunnel underpinning my world.

At Nanpean Cemetery we fan out, amateur sleuths
hunting down uncles. But here, in this sky-soaked mausoleum,

what feels like half of the stones bear our name,
so many Allens the word is unhinged

and we are on a slope of shifting sun-baked china clay.
As you fill in the dates of your home-made family tree

all we can do, your urban offspring,
is repeat the phrases you offered us in youth

and then left to settle, their roots bedding in:
Well lads, believe me, this is where we're from!

Song for Billy MacKenzie

I dreamt I saw you still alive,
walking your dogs on Broughty Ferry,
Heaven streaming out of your eyes
as it always did, before you left us.

You sang a song about the moon,
how it shines on lovers and fools,
and how that light leads them too soon
behind the curl of the harbour wall,

up to the summit of Dundee Law,
which once was a torch of liquid fire,
the same fire that found itself in you,
a cold, glistening tongue that flared.

It burned so hard it set you free
to sing of Heaven, its towers, its hills,
eternal beaches, one infinite street
where glamorous men meet glamorous girls,

and you have appropriate songs to sing,
matching the breathless heights you reached,
songs that leave us satisfied,
and you with your dogs on this moonlit beach.

The Art of Gardening

for Matthew

There will be enough of those who say go slow,
be moderate, think before you speak,
do not rock the boat you find yourself in,
never say no to a leg up or money,
enough who will counsel caution,
acquiescence to the norm, who will try
to sell you the ethics of a chameleon,
subservience to the gods of cliché,
enough who will preach the logic of slavery,
the tongue-tied, twisted rhetoric of obeisance,
purveyors of common-sense and natural law,
enough agents of the common books of prayer,
hackneyed rhymers, exhausted primers,
much more than enough. So now, my son,
let's imagine we are two rounded stones,
well used to the weight of water passing over,
oblivious to anything that would stick,
and here, unseen, unnoticed, undisturbed,
in a place of high walls and ancient trees,
let me tell you what this life is all about:
be brave but steady, be wild but sane,
be social but selective, wise beyond learning,
say no to the world so often and so loudly
that the world stops insisting that you agree,
say no to the world but keep your yeses safe
for yourself and the few true friends you find.
Grow those yeses in secret, bide your time,
grow hard to the tongues of those that distrust you,
till what you know and what you want
and, most of all, what you can in the end imagine,
after all lessons, all sacrifice, all knowledge,
all the tired topoi of each weary preceptor,
has grown under your care to the size of a garden,

full of the plants and flowers you designed,
exotic and familiar habitable spheres,
tend them in secret until you have made
somewhere you can invite the world to visit,
somewhere you can call your home.

How to Improve your Sleep

Leave your job, get divorced, put your children
into care, move to a countryside cottage
on another continent, break all relations
with your mother and father, do not pass on
your new address to your siblings, eradicate
all memories after the age of five.
Do not smoke, drink, or harbour ambitions,
on no account attempt to write poetry.
Eat four hours before going to bed.
Do not think about your own mortality.
Pray if it helps, but don't if it doesn't.
Masturbate only when you feel drowsy.
Put all stimulating literature away.
Take nothing but unsweetened biscuits,
unleavened bread and absurd, outlandish
teas, like *Chamomile, Dill and Pigeon-Dust.*
Eat nothing sweet, avoid all conversations.
Buy a moulded bed and a wrap-around
stereo, avoid all popular music.
Try not to dream, but, if you must, forget each one
as quickly as you can; avoid all news.
On retiring wear comfortable, ugly pyjamas
and bed-socks. Do not wash, avoid all mirrors.
Try to imagine yourself as a small stone
in the company of a billion other small stones
under a huge, impassable mountain-range
at the very bottom of the ocean.

The Purpose of Love Poetry in Twenty-First Century Ireland

In the driveway of the 357th house
on the 599th abandoned ghost estate,
where no car has ever driven
and no human eye will ever say goodbye,
where no photographs will ever be snapped
or surprise birthday party spill outside,
where no birds sit on drying hydrangeas
and no postmen anticipate waiting dogs,
where no meter readings will ever be taken
or quick illicit kisses ever be snatched,
where rain splashes thick on unwashed concrete
and urban wolves search in vain for food,
where rats scurry out from mud-clogged drains
and hungry crows peck between drab-coloured slabs,
where snails inch out from sodden gutters
and nothing disturbs the keening of the wind . . . .

the welcoming shade of the Japanese knotweed.

Rossbeigh

for Breeda and Kevin

The bundle of swimmer's clothes
turns into a beached dolphin,

sunlight streaks the curves
of its sleek alien skin,

its snout is a fastened zip,
glistening razor-wire,

on its back an orange hole
the size of an elephant's eye.

It is a black hole consuming
matter till it sprouts,

one of Van Gogh's sunflowers
turned inside out.

I put the hell mouth
inside my phone and left.

Months later I saw,
how could I have missed,

a pancake stone monument,
a childish headstone,

complete with twig antenna,
E.T. phoning home.

Parkinson's Disease

for Roy Sellars

There is a rhythm to this
you must accept.
Something broken

and yet of itself.
Involuntary action,
a mad shake and pulse

of your hand,
your arm,
as if your brain was catching music,

some subtle drumbeat
nobody else can hear.
You are possessed

by something other
than you can fully own,
volatile ghost,

foreign body,
a force that has stolen
your stance,

amused
to transform you,
puppet

with entangled strings,
controlled by clumsy
fingers.

Still, for all this,
you ride the wave,
abiding,

steering as steady a path
as you can
through the turbulence.

An old sea lag,
lashed tightly
to the mast,

crying for release
as the sirens sing,
a traveller,

bent double by his load,
hoping that the lights
ahead are no mirage.

To the Socket

for Carrie

I dreamt of a woman like her,
the nape of her neck was smooth as marble,
her fingers were sweet smelling flowers,
her smile was the moon breaking through clouds,
the earth echoed under her feet,
her breasts were satin-white lilies,
her eyes mysterious birds,
and as she began to sing to me,
the tilt of the earth corrected itself,
spring and summer re-established their hold,
and death shrank back into his cave,
falling into a dreamless sleep.

She is as beautiful to my eyes
as an early frost on Hampstead Heath,
evening birdsong on Westminster Bridge,
the Thames as the morning sun peeps through
clouds that take its pinkish glint
and gift still sleepy commuters with
a hint of Blake's rejuvenated town.
Her face is like a citadel
built in the name of the glory of God,
beyond dispute, beyond conflict,
created evidence, full sign
of what he called the Human Face Divine.

I somehow lost her and could not find her
and so I wandered the streets at night,
strange patterns rippled the darkness
then shot across deserted streets.
When I looked up the moon was spinning,
a maniacal Catherine Wheel,
bits of mountain and crater edges
snapping off into eccentric orbits.

A piece crashed onto the distant hillside,
a drawing-pin discarded
from the writing table of the gods.

I could not sleep because of thoughts of her,
the sweet dissymmetry of her eyes
held me suspended between night and day,
her lips, neither real nor wholly imagined,
coiled tighter the chord of love in my heart,
and I wanted to reach out to her,
touch her bare shoulders, her neck,
run my fingers across her right cheek-bone,
and press her body close to mine.
I knew she was waiting patiently for me
in a dream sprung deep inside my mind,
but I could not sleep because of thoughts of her.

A fire spread throughout my life,
my dreams became a heap of cinders,
floating but dead, weightless remainders,
spent of all fuel, all future, all connection,
all tales that can be told, all avenues back,
and as the wind picked them up, frantic sparks,
in mockery of the flames that made them,
they covered in a film the image of her face,
caking it into a stone idol, as if some hand
other than my own had fashioned her,
eyeless, coldly conscious, universally visible,
waiting for that one enchanted kiss.

Torn

Now we are lost
to each other
and you live in
that place of skulls
where no one laughs
and the seas roar
lamentations
and I remain
in the warmth of
your parents' house
learning the songs
you sang as a
girl reading the books
you learnt by heart
eating the food
that raised you,
I wonder how
destiny comes
to separate
what we have made
and why things
which should stand true
turn inside out.

I have written
a poem set
against the wind
that washes us
to different shores,
it folds us back
as poems can
against the clock
and compass face.
It folds us back
as poems can
into that realm

time denies us.
Like a song sung
by an old drunk
at a wedding,
it folds us back.
Like a song heard
by the harbour
wall at midnight
by a woman half mad,
it folds us back.
Like a child hears
another child's mother
singing it to sleep,
it folds us back.
As poems can
and sometimes will,
it folds us back.

Something in You Remains Completed

for Sarah Wood

Let this be, let this one thought stand.
The sun dies every day it is born,
tears fall and are not replaced,
time cracks open the thickest masonry,

every atom swerves, inclines to its end,
but something in you resists, intact,
against all law and every sentence,
against the measure and slant of things,

contrapuntal to the fact of life,
death, being, and mutability,
like a song overheard from another world,

like a stone gathers all things to itself,
like a question no one ever thought to ask,
something in you remains completed.

Bright Star, Elegy for David Bowie

His lips recoil from the taste of the real.
His eyes look through to the earliest stars.

Outside your mind is his best imagining,
he has paved our footpath with tiny pearls.

He smokes his cigarette like an ivory pen,
his fingers caressing the shoulders of ghosts.

He wears his suit like a mannequin would,
only with more perpetual purpose.

Beyond his profile down by the lakeside,
where heavenly metal pianos play,

angels in fur coats stand to attention
as the skies collapse into orange flame.

The man with the clipboard said he was dead
and all of our colours faded to dust.

The shrill pantheon of matinee gods
shrugged their shoulders, as if passing the buck.

Everyone wept and put stones in their mouths.
News men and news women read elegiac verse.

The internet stuck up a tearful emoticon
and old men buried their hands in the earth.

Far away beyond blue-filtered shorelines,
where devils leaf through prohibited texts

and children dance at midnight unattended,
his spirit rose like a passing comet.

And we said, as all the museums caught fire
and politicians wept into their fists,

he is as far beyond us now as he ever was,
bright star making a halo of the darkness.

We could hear the new music of the spheres.
You can listen to his eternity from here.

It says:

Do everything with joy.
Do everything with love.
Do everything as if the world was still fixable.
Raise your head above the crowd,
then help the crowd to rise up too.
Smile brilliantly into the future.
Smile brilliantly at the camera of your death.
Imitate the life of the sun.
Imitate the lives of the moon.
Honestly face your demons down.
Shine like a light that has no source
save for its own irrepressible desires.
Invent a galaxy you can live in.
Reinvent what it means to have a face.
Burn brightly. Burn beautifully.
Burn through the inconvenience of time.
Burn through the inadequacies of space.
Burn through the lone splendours of philosophy.
Burn like every fresh-faced new kid on the block.
Burn like the force that sweeps through the universe.
Burn your way back to the star-stuff that made you.
Burn like the singular point of all energy.
Burn like an absolute image of release.

The Spells

after P. B. Shelley

Start over. Start again. Rise up
from your latest defeat,
imitate the moon. Reopen your eyes
and look beyond this debris.
Grow new wings. Lengthen your stride.
Where Empire resumes resume
yourself. Redouble your efforts.
Work until work itself is redeemed
and the very last Pimp pays back
the last penny he stole from the poor,
and the poor are all forgiveness. Start over.
Start again. Push the bankers and their
poisonous apologists into the freezing
ocean. Claw back your taxes
from the military. Return mothers to their
children. Recall all fathers to the practice
of patience. Close down the asylums.
Once again bury the smart guns
and nightmare bombs in bunkers
underneath the deepest mountains.
Release yourselves from endless waves
of irony and studied disaffection.
Disarm, disengage the soldier of his arsenal,
decommission, decontaminate, demob.
Take every school and fill it with teachers.
Take each library and open all its doors.
Start over. Start again. Create.
Create even before Hope has arrived.
Initiate a new age, elect prophets.
Sack professional technocratic gangsters.
Close down quangos. Silence the tribunals.
Break open the prisons. Start over.
Start again. Imitate the moon,
which even in defeat plans its newest

recovery. Fiercely promote the wise.
Celebrate the elderly. Restore
the big cats to their habitats.
Reforest the deserts. Leave the oil
pooling under the rocks. Let the birds
and the fishes breed their way back
into their full dominion on earth.
Close down the stock exchanges.
Give access to health care for free.
Abolish copyright, careerism, cancer.
Fund research into cures for violence.
Roll up all the flags. Give empty houses
to the homeless. Give empty tower blocks
back to the people. Facilitate
the building of bridges, hospitals,
art centres and skate parks. Down
tools, skip work, and head out to the west.
Start over. Start again. Breed geniuses,
visionaries, poets, carers, play-actors,
comics, philosophers, scientists, translators.
Procreate. Multiply yourselves into
sustainable self-governing communes.
Save Literature from the cinema. Save cinema
from mobile phones. Save conversation
from the social network. Save spirituality
from Churches and Preachers. Liberate
once again, after failure and betrayals.
Unbind again, shake your chains in the face
of certain defeat. Imitate the moon.
Remember like it you are indestructible.
Recall that in the end and whenever the worst
threatens to return and wreck your world,
everything you have managed to build,
you can once again, and as if
for the very first time, in a glorious flare
and loop of self-renewal, start over. Start again.

About the Author

Graham Allen is Professor in English in UCC and has had his poetry published in numerous journals. He was the winner of the 2010 Listowel Single Poem Prize and has been short-listed for various other prizes, including the Crashaw Prize in 2014 and the Strong/Shine First Collection Prize 2015. He was one of the featured poets in the *Poetry Ireland Review* April 2016 issue on *The Rising Generation* and in Poetry Ireland's promotion of 2016's Poetry Day. His e-poem *Holes* and his collection *The One That Got Away* (2014) are also published by New Binary Press.

Lightning Source UK Ltd.
Milton Keynes UK
UKOW04f1050190716

278720UK00001B/1/P